America's
National Parks, Monuments & Memorials

impact
PHOTO·GRAPHICS

Impact, 4961 Windplay Drive, El Dorado Hills, CA 95762

Photographers – Bob Clemenz Photography, Craig Blacklock/Larry Ulrich Stock Photography, James Blank, Dick Dietrich/Dietrich, Leis Stock Photography, J. Scott Graham, Peter Gridley, Mark Henderson, Dai Hirota, George H. H. Huey, Ron Maurer, Robin Miller/NPS, William Neill/Larry Ulrich Stock Photography, Glenn Van Ninwegen, Jon Ortner, Laurence Parent, Robert Thayer, David Thoresen, Larry Ulrich, John Wagner

ISBN-10: 1-60068-011-9
ISBN-13: 978-1-60068-011-9

First Printing, August 2006

impact
PHOTO·GRAPHICS ®

4961 Windplay Drive, El Dorado Hills, CA 95762
www.impactphotographics.com

Printed in China

America's
National Parks, Monuments & Memorials

The National Park System truly began with the establishment of Yellowstone National Park in 1872. Several other areas had been set aside earlier by the U.S. government to ensure their preservation, including Hot Springs, Arkansas in 1832 and Yosemite Valley, which was ceded to the state of California in 1864. For that matter, the northern tip of Cape Cod was initially set aside as the "Province Lands" by the Plymouth Colony in the early 1600's. However, Yellowstone was the first area specifically established through legislation as a National Park.

The Passage of the Antiquities Act of 1906 brought about another means of creating National Park areas. The act allowed the President of the United States to set aside significant areas located on federal land as National Monuments.

Enjoy viewing some of the most popular National Parks, Monuments and Memorials throughout the United States.

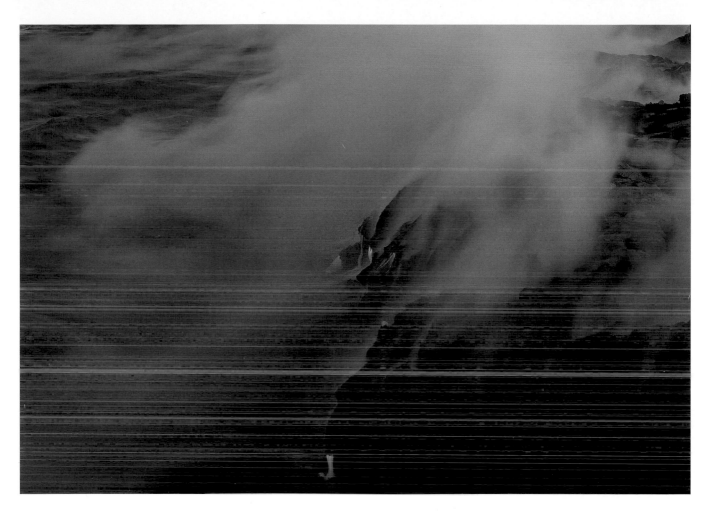

Hawai'i Volcanoes National Park, Hawai'i

Hawai'i Volcanoes National Park displays the results of 70 million years of volcanism, migration, and evolution – processes that thrust a bare land from the sea and clothed it with complex and unique ecosystems and a distinct human culture.

Haleakalā National Park, Hawai‘i

Haleakala National Park vibrates with stories of ancient and modern Hawaiian culture and protects the bond between the land and its people. A visit to this special place will renew your spirit of adventure amid stark volcanic landscapes, sub-tropical rain forest and the unforgettable experience of hiking the backcountry.

USS *Arizona* National Memorial, Hawai'i

Wakes of a tour boat are left behind as it pulls away with visitors from the USS *Arizona* Memorial. Constructed in 1961, the memorial was dedicated on Memorial Day 1962 and became a unit of the National Park Service in 1980.

Denali National Park & Preserve, Alaska

It's more than a mountain. Denali National Park & Preserve features North America's highest mountain, 20,320-foot tall Mount McKinley.

Cabrillo National Monument, California

Cabrillo National Monument offers a superb view of San Diego's harbor and skyline. At the highest point of the park stands the Old Point Loma Lighthouse, which has been a San Diego icon since 1854.

Joshua Tree National Park, California

The higher Mojave Desert and the lower Colorado Desert are two large ecosystems that come together at Joshua Tree National Park. Five fan palm oases also dot the park, indicating those few areas where water occurs naturally and wildlife abounds.

Death Valley National Park, California
The unique wildlife, geology, archeology, and the colorful historical events of Death Valley and the Mojave Preserve attract scientists and enthusiasts from all over the world.

Kings Canyon National Park, California

Kings Canyon is home to giants: immense mountains, deep canyons, and huge trees. Thanks to its extensive elevational range, this park protects stunningly diverse habitats.

Sequoia National Park, California

Sequoia National Park is the second-oldest national park in the United States. It was established in 1890 to protect the Big Trees in the Giant Forest, including the General Sherman Tree, the world's largest living thing.

Yosemite National Park, California

Yosemite National Park embraces these major attractions: alpine wilderness, three groves of Giant Sequoias and the glacially carved Yosemite Valley with impressive waterfalls, cliffs and unusual rock formations.

Muir Woods National Monument, California

"This is the best tree-lovers monument that could possibly be found in all the forests of the world," declared conservationist John Muir when describing the majestic coast redwoods of Muir Woods.

Redwood National & State Parks, California

Redwood National and State Parks are home to some of the world's tallest trees: old-growth coast redwoods. They can live to be 2,000 years old and grow to over 300 feet tall. Spruce, hemlock, Douglas-fir, berry bushes, sword ferns and rhododendron create a multiple canopied understory that towers over all visitors.

Crater Lake National Park, Oregon

"All ingenuity of nature seems to have been exerted to the fullest capacity to build a grand awe-inspiring temple the likes of which the world has never seen before," said William G. Steel, the founding father of Crater Lake National Park.

Mount St. Helens National Volcanic Monument, Washington

On May 18, 1980, an earthquake measuring 5.1 on the Richter scale caused Mount St. Helens to erupt. The eruption lasted nine hours, and with it Mount St. Helens and the surrounding landscape were dramatically changed.

Mount Rainier National Park, Washington

Welcome to a mountain wonderland famous for dense forests, dazzling wildflower meadows, tremendous snowfields, rugged glaciers, and an active volcano.

Olympic National Park, Washington

Within Olympic National Park, one will find Pacific beaches, rainforest valleys, glacier-capped peaks and a stunning variety of plants and animals. Much of Olympic National Park is blanketed in forests. From wind-sculpted subalpine firs at treeline, to towering Sitka spruce in the rain forest, this park nurtures some of the finest primeval forests in the country.

Saguaro National Park, Arizona
Saguaro National Park invites you to "Experience Your America" in a way that only the Sonoran Desert can offer. This unique desert is home to the most recognizable cactus in the world, the majestic saguaro.

Montezuma Castle National Monument, Arizona

This five-story, 20 room cliff dwelling nestled into a limestone recess high above Beaver Creek served as a "high-rise apartment building" for prehistoric Sinagua Indians over 600 years ago. It is one of the best preserved cliff dwellings in North America.

Grand Canyon National Park, Arizona

One of the most spectacular examples of erosion anywhere in the world, the Grand Canyon is unmatched in the incomparable vistas it offers to visitors on all rims – North, South, East and West.

Petrified Forest National Park, Arizona

Petrified Forest National Park features one of the world's largest and most colorful concentrations of petrified wood, the multi-hued badlands, historic structures, archeological sites, and displays of 225 million year old fossils.

Zion National Park, Utah

Zion National Park encompasses some of the most scenic canyon country in the United States. The park is characterized by high plateaus, a maze of narrow, deep, sandstone canyons and striking rock towers and mesas.

Bryce Canyon National Park, Utah

Bryce Canyon National Park is named for one of a series of horseshoe-shaped amphitheaters carved from the eastern edge of the Paunsaugunt Plateau in southern Utah.

Capitol Reef National Park, Utah

Capitol Reef National Park was established to protect the grand Waterpocket Fold, colorful geologic features, as well as the unique historical and cultural history found in the area.

Arches National Park, Utah

Arches National Park preserves over two thousand natural sandstone arches, including the world-famous Delicate Arch, in addition to a variety of unique geological resources and formations.

Canyonlands National Park, Utah

Canyonlands National Park preserves an amazing colorful landscape of sedimentary sandstones eroded into countless canyons, mesas and buttes by the Colorado River and its tributaries.

Natural Bridges National Monument, Utah

Natural Bridges protects some of the finest examples of ancient stone architecture in the southwest. Located on a tree-covered mesa cut by deep sandstone canyons, three natural bridges formed where meandering streams eroded the canyon walls.

Dinosaur National Monument, Colorado and Utah

Dinosaur National Monument is the legacy of rivers, past and present. Here, preserved in the sands of an ancient river, is a time capsule from the world of dinosaurs. The dinosaur quarry discovered here by Earl Douglas in 1909 has yielded the bones of 10 species of "terrible lizards" that lived millions of years ago.

Mesa Verde National Park, Colorado

Mesa Verde, Spanish for "green table", offers an unparalleled opportunity to see and experience a unique cultural and physical landscape. Cliff Palace, the largest cliff dwelling in North America, was home to the Anasazi people.

Colorado National Monument, Colorado
Colorado National Monument preserves one of the grand landscapes of the American West with sheer-walled canyons, towering monoliths, colorful formations and diverse wildlife.

Rocky Mountain National Park, Colorado

Established on January 26, 1915, Rocky Mountain National Park is a living showcase of the grandeur of the Rocky Mountains. From wet, grassy valleys to the weather-ravaged top of Longs Peak, a visitor to the park has opportunities for countless breath-taking experiences and adventures.

Great Sand Dunes National Park & Preserve, Colorado

Nestled in southern Colorado, North America's tallest dunes rise over 750 feet high against the rugged
Sangre de Cristo Mountains. The wind-shaped dunes glow beneath the rugged backdrop of the mountains.

31

Grand Teton National Park, Wyoming
Located in northwestern Wyoming, Grand Teton National Park protects stunning mountain scenery and a diverse array of wildlife with the Teton Range as the central feature.

Upper Geyser Basin, Yellowstone National Park, Wyoming, Montana, and Idaho

This is the premier outpost in the world for observing active geysers. Nowhere else compares to the remarkable collection of subterranean vents, which pipe up hot water from beneath the surface of the earth.

Devils Tower National Monument, Wyoming

Devils Tower has long been a beacon, attracting people and capturing their imaginations since prehistoric times. The nearly vertical monolith rises 1,267 feet above the meandering Belle Fourche River.

Glacier National Park, Montana

Created in 1910, Glacier National Park provides over one million acres of habitat and protection for a wonderful variety of wildlife and wildflowers. The spectacular glaciated landscape is a hiker's paradise, containing 700 miles of maintained trails.

Carlsbad Caverns National Park, New Mexico

Established to preserve Carlsbad Cavern and numerous other caves within a Permian-age fossil reef, the park contains more than 100 known caves, including Lechuguilla Cave.

Guadalupe National Park, Texas

The evening sun rests on the western face of the Guadalupe Mountains. Rising from the desert, this mountain mass contains portions of the world's most extensive and significant Permian limestone fossil reef.

Big Bend National Park, Texas

Big Bend includes massive canyons, vast desert expanses, and the entire Chisos Mountain Range. Here, you can explore one of the last remaining wild corners of the United States and experience unmatched sights, sounds, and solitude.

Mt. Rushmore National Memorial, South Dakota

George Washington, Thomas Jefferson, Abraham Lincoln, and Theodore Roosevelt laid a foundation for the
United States of America as solid as the rock from which their figures were carved.

Badlands National Park, South Dakota
Located in southwestern South Dakota, Badlands National Park consists of sharply eroded buttes, pinnacles and spires blended with the largest protected mixed grass prairie in the United States.

Theodore Roosevelt National Park, North Dakota

The colorful North Dakota Badlands provides the scenic backdrop to Theodore Roosevelt National Park. The Little Missouri River has shaped this land which is home to a variety of plants and animals.

Jefferson National Expansion Memorial, Missouri
Jefferson National Expansion Memorial, designed by architect Eero Saarinen, consists of the Gateway Arch,
the Museum of Westward Expansion, and St. Louis' Old Courthouse.

Mammoth Cave National Park, Kentucky

With over 350 miles of surveyed caves, Mammoth Cave is at least three times longer than any other cave system in the world.

Everglades National Park, Florida

Spanning the southern tip of the Florida peninsula and most of Florida Bay, Everglades National Park is the
only subtropical preserve in North America.

Great Smoky Mountains National Park, Tennessee and North Carolina
The Great Smoky Mountains are named for the rising streamers of mist and soft blue haze which so frequently veil the valleys and ridges of the range. Over seven feet of annual rainfall and 500,000 acres of lush forest fuel the characteristic vapors.

Shenandoah National Park, Virginia

Shenandoah National Park lies astride a beautiful section of the Blue Ridge Mountains, which form the eastern rampart of the Appalachian Mountains between Pennsylvania and Georgia.

Arlington National Cemetery, Virginia

Entombed in 1921, a World War I *"American Soldier known but to God"* rests beneath this marble memorial. Resting beside him are unknown soldiers from World War II and the Korean War. Sentinels of the elite Third U.S. Infantry guard the Tomb of the Unknowns 24 hours a day.

The National Mall, Washington, DC

The Washington Monument honors those who helped the 13 colonies become one nation, while the Lincoln Memorial remembers those who preserved that Union at great sacrifice. The Capitol serves as living testimony to the enduring principles that still govern this country.

Gettysburg National Military Park, Pennsylvania
Located 50 miles northwest of Baltimore, the small town of Gettysburg, Pennsylvania was the site of the largest battle ever waged during the American Civil War. It now includes over 1,400 monuments, markers and memorials.

Liberty Bell, Independence National Historic Park, Pennsylvania

Originally hung in the tower of the new State House (Independence Hall) in Philadelphia in 1753, the Liberty Bell rang out on important occasions. Today, the bell is a revered symbol of freedom.

Statue of Liberty National Monument, New York and New Jersey

Located on Liberty Island in New York Harbor, the Statue of Liberty was a gift of international friendship from the people of France to the people of the United States and is one of the more universal symbols of political freedom and democracy.

Acadia National Park, Maine
Located on the rugged coast of Maine, Acadia National Park encompasses over 47,000 acres of granite-domed mountains, woodlands, lakes, and ocean shoreline.